PET REPTILES

Leon Gray

Grolier
an imprint of

www.scholastic.com/librarypublishing

Published 2009 by Grolier
An Imprint of Scholastic Library Publishing
Old Sherman Turnpike
Danbury, Connecticut 06816

For The Brown Reference Group plc
Project Editor: Jolyon Goddard
Picture Researchers: Clare Newman, Sophie
Mortimer
Designer: Sarah Williams
Managing Editor: Tim Harris

Volume ISBN-13: 978-0-7172-8051-3
Volume ISBN-10: 0-7172-8051-9

**Library of Congress
Cataloging-in-Publication Data**

Nature's children. Set 5.
    p. cm.
  Includes index.
  ISBN-13: 978-0-7172-8084-1
  ISBN-10: 0-7172-8084-5 (set)
  1. Animals--Encyclopedias, Juvenile. I.
Grolier (Firm)
  QL49.N386 2009
  590.3--dc22
                        2008014674

Printed and bound in China

PICTURE CREDITS

Front Cover: **Shutterstock**: Lori Martin.

Back Cover: **Shutterstock**: R.L. Hambley,
Ovidiu Iordachi, Cathy Keifer.

Corbis: Joson 21; **NaturePL**: Ingo Arndt
42, John Cancalosi 30, 34, Tony Phelps 41;
Shutterstock: Peter Baxter 46, Rusty
Dodson 9, Joy Fera 10, R.L. Hambley 14,
Innocent 2–3, Elpis Ioannidis 29, Julie Keen
18, Cathy Keifer 13, 26–27, Dolores Lin
45, Mashe 5, Ismael Montero Verdu 6,
Objectsforall 4, Jason Osborne 17,
A. Paterson 37, PhotoSky4t.com 38,
Mikko Pitkanen 22; **Still Pictures**: Michel
Gunther 33.

Contents

FACT FILE: Pet Reptiles

Class	Reptiles (Reptilia)
Orders	Lizards and snakes (Squamata); turtles, tortoises, and terrapins (Testudines)
Families	Several families
Genera	Various genera
Species	Common pet reptiles include the green iguana (*Iguana iguana*), corn snake (*Elaphe guttata*), and common slider (*Trachemys scripta*)
World distribution	Pet reptiles are popular worldwide; wild reptiles are found on every continent except Antarctica
Habitat	Pet reptiles should be kept in a cage or glass tank with plants, rocks, or sand; wild reptiles live in many places, such as deserts, forests, rivers, and oceans
Distinctive physical characteristics	Reptiles come in a range of sizes; some have four legs, others have none; they have dry, scaly skin, which is shed as they grow
Habits	Reptiles are cold-blooded and need heat to warm up their body; wild reptiles bask in the sun to keep warm; pet reptiles need a basking lamp or heating pad
Diet	Depends on the species—plants or animals

Introduction

The class of animals known as reptiles has a bad reputation. Many people are afraid of snakes and lizards. But reptiles are fascinating creatures. In fact, most reptiles are harmless and do well in **captivity**, even in people's homes. Various types of snakes, lizards, and turtles make excellent pets. Some of the larger kinds of reptiles can live as long as 40 years or more.

Chameleons (KAH-MEEL-EE-UNZ) can change their skin color to suit their mood, to hide themselves, or to attract a mate.

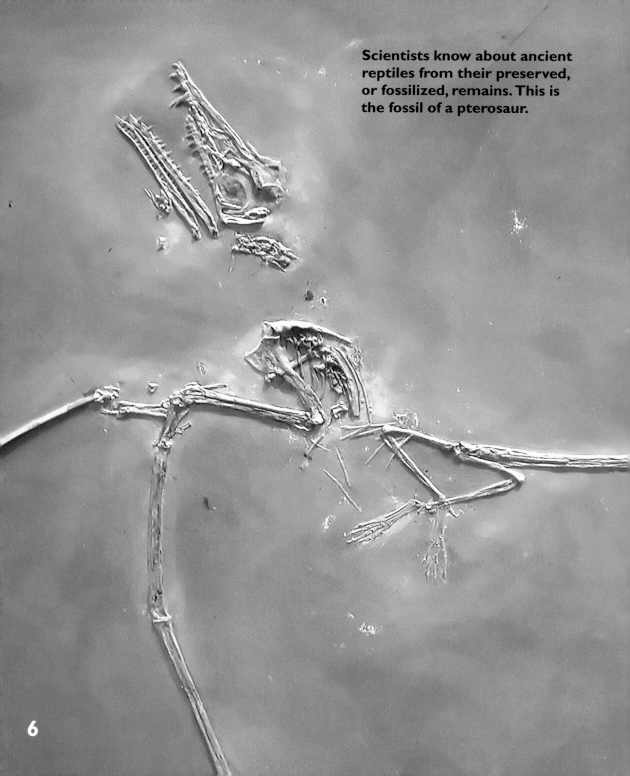

Scientists know about ancient reptiles from their preserved, or fossilized, remains. This is the fossil of a pterosaur.

Reptile Relations

Reptiles have been around for a very long time. Between 280 and 65 million years ago, reptiles ruled the world. The most famous of these ancient reptiles were the dinosaurs. However, there were also flying reptiles called pterosaurs (TER-UH-SORZ) and reptiles that lived in the sea called ichthyosaurs (IK-THEE-UH-SORZ) and plesiosaurs (PLEE-SEE-UH-SORZ).

Reptiles from ancient times, such as dinosaurs, have long since died out. Modern reptiles come in many different shapes and sizes. There are fierce **predators** such as saltwater crocodiles and anaconda snakes. There are also color-changing lizards called chameleons, the lizardlike tuatara (TOO-UH-TAR-UH) from New Zealand, and the shelled turtles. Like many other animals, reptiles have a heart to pump blood through their body, and they break down the food they eat in their digestive system. Unlike mammals, such as cats, dogs, and humans, reptiles are cold-blooded and **bask** in sunlight to keep warm. They also have dry, scaly skin, which they shed as they grow.

7

Bad Reputation

Some people fear reptiles. But most reptiles would rather run—or slither—away and hide than harm a person. And most give warnings before attacking. A rattlesnake rattles its tail as a warning before it strikes. Many poisonous snakes are brightly colored to warn other animals that they are dangerous. Most reptiles, however, are harmless. There are only two poisonous lizards. They are the Mexican beaded lizard and the Gila (HEE-LUH) monster. Of the 2,700 **species**, or types, of snakes in the world, about 500 are poisonous. But only about 40 species are dangerous enough to kill a human.

The Gila monster is a poisonous lizard that lives in the southwestern United States and northern Mexico. It grows to about 2 feet (60 cm) long.

Bearded dragons are popular pet reptiles. They originate from Australia and can grow to 2 feet (60 cm).

Reptiles as Pets

Many people like to keep reptiles as pets. Lizards and snakes are the most popular. But not all reptiles make good pets. Wild reptiles should never be taken as pets. They are likely to be aggressive and hard to handle. They also carry diseases and **parasites** that can harm other pets. Large reptiles, such as iguanas and pythons, need a lot of space and a lot of attention from their owners. Most people prefer to keep smaller reptiles as pets because they are easier to house and feed. It is best to keep away from poisonous reptiles unless you are an expert reptile owner!

Popular Lizards

One of the most popular pet lizards is the leopard gecko. These friendly creatures love to be handled, and they do not bite. They can be housed in a fairly small glass tank—10 to 15 gallons (38 to 57 l) is usually big enough. Sand, rocks, and small logs should be added to the tank to help the leopard gecko settle into its new home. It will also need a small basking lamp or heating pad under the tank. That will help the lizard keep its body warm. Another popular pet is the green anole (UH-NO-LEE). This lizard thrives in a similar environment to the leopard gecko, but it will need a few climbing branches and an **ultraviolet** lamp to complete its home.

Leopard geckos are found naturally in Asia. Unlike many other types of geckos, leopard geckos have eyelids.

Ball pythons are the smallest of the African pythons. When they feel threatened, these snakes curl up into a ball.

14

Keeping Snakes

Snakes make excellent pets. Corn snakes are one of the best reptile pets for new owners because they are friendly and easy to care for. Corn snakes grow up to 5 feet (1.5 m) long. They can live comfortably in a standard glass tank. Corn snakes need a layer of shredded paper or wood shavings on the bottom of their tank. They also need a "hide box" to help them feel safe.

Ball pythons are another popular pet snake. Ball pythons can live comfortably in a 20-gallon (76-l) glass tank with a heating pad and a hide box. It is important to buy a ball python from a pet store that is well known for the quality of the animals it sells. Ball pythons that have been taken from the wild and are not used to being handled by humans might not eat the food offered to them. They can also be aggressive if taken from the wild.

Pet Turtles

Turtles are often sold in pet stores. They include terrapins—a name often used to describe turtles that live in freshwater—and tortoises, or land turtles. Tropical species may be very expensive, but some common turtles, such as red-eared sliders and **aquatic** barking turtles, can be very affordable. It is important to do your homework before buying a turtle. Many people don't realize how much care these reptiles need. Aquatic turtles are especially demanding since they need a complicated setup of heaters, ultraviolet lights, and water filters to survive in captivity.

A tortoise's tough shell protects it from enemies in the wild. Unlike other types of turtles, most tortoises cannot swim.

17

A sick pet water
dragon receives an
injection of medicine
from a vet.

In Good Health

The first sign of a healthy reptile is bright,
clean eyes. The mouth should also be free from
infected areas, or **abscesses**. Before choosing
a pet reptile, run your hands along the body
of the reptile to check for lumps and bruises.
One disease to watch out for is mouthrot. This
common reptile disease occurs when the animal
rubs its nose against the sides of its enclosure. It
is a common sign that the reptile is being housed
in an enclosure that is too small.

Homemaking

Most pet reptiles live in a glass tank with a screen top. This type of enclosure is easy to clean and offers a clear view of the animal inside. Other pet reptiles, such as iguanas, can live in barred cages. The size of the cage or tank depends on the size of the reptile. Swift-moving and **arboreal**, or tree-dwelling, reptiles need a large cage so they have plenty of room to climb and move around. Reptiles that are naturally found in deserts need a tank with sand and rocks. Tropical snakes and lizards will need a lot of greenery, or foliage.

It is important to secure the top of the tank, because large reptiles can force open the lid to escape. Cage clips or **bungee cords** are the best way to keep large pet reptiles inside their home.

Even though Gila monsters are poisonous, they very rarely bite humans.

21

A wild green iguana warms up in the morning sunshine.

Heating the Tank

Reptiles are cold-blooded animals. In the wild, they need to bask in sunlight to warm up and stay healthy. As pets, reptiles also need a source of light to control their body temperature. Most owners use a basking lamp or heating pad to give the reptile the heat that it needs. Basking lamps heat the reptile from above. The reptile sits under the basking lamp to warm up. When it is warm enough, the reptile moves off to find shelter. Most basking lamps are controlled by a timer, so the reptile does not get too hot. Heating pads also keep a pet reptile warm. The pads are placed inside or underneath the cage or tank.

The light cycle of the basking lamp should match the amount of light a reptile would get in the wild. Many reptile owners use electronic timers to match the natural daylight cycle of the year. There are also electronic devices available from pet stores that measure the amount of natural light—for example, coming through windows—and adjust the lighting inside the reptile's cage or tank.

Cleaning the Cage

Reptiles that live in a dirty cage or tank will get sick and might even die. It is very important to keep the cage or tank as clean as possible. Cleaning the cage or tank once a week should be enough.

A simple glass tank should be wiped with a clean sponge or towel. Household cleaners contain harmful chemicals that can poison a reptile, so it is best to use a special glass cleaner for reptile tanks. The **litter** at the bottom of the tank should be changed and the reptile's water bottle refilled frequently. If the cage or tank contains plants, branches, logs, or ornaments, these also need to be wiped clean.

Day or Night

Many pet reptiles are active during the day and sleep at night. These kinds of animals are called **diurnal** (DI-UR-NUL). Green iguanas, chameleons, tortoises, common sliders are diurnal. Other reptiles rest during the day and are active at night. These creatures are called **nocturnal**. Nocturnal reptiles include many types of geckos and certain snakes, such as ball pythons and corn snakes. Snakes often will not move—sometimes for days—after eating a big meal, too.

Wild reptiles that live in regions where the winters are cold spend winter in a deep sleeplike state. In this state, their body processes are slowed and their body temperature is lowered. This condition is called **hibernation**. The reptile wakes up in spring when the weather is warmer and food is plentiful. Pet reptiles, especially those kept indoors in tanks, generally do not hibernate. However, pet tortoises might still hibernate through winter. A hibernating tortoise should be placed in a box lined with towels or filled with straw and checked regularly.

A pet leopard gecko prepares to snatch a fly as it passes.

Feeding Time

It is important to find out what kind of food a pet reptile needs to eat to stay healthy. Many reptiles are **herbivores**. Herbivores eat only plant matter, such as fruits and vegetables. Others are **carnivores**. Carnivores eat mostly other animals. Most carnivorous reptiles must be fed living animals. Some eat insects, such as crickets. Larger reptiles eat rodents, such as mice or rats. Some reptiles are **omnivores** and eat both plants and animals.

Many reptile owners notice that their pets have favorite foods. A new pet reptile should be fed a variety of different foods to find out its preferences. Pet stores sell most kinds of reptile foods. It can be expensive feeding a large reptile, so many owners collect wild insects or breed their own mice or rats to feed their pet.

Tortoises are plant eaters and will eat many kinds of fruits and vegetables, including tomatoes.

29

Corn snakes are popular pets. Wild corn snakes live in the United States and hunt mice and rats.

Handling Reptiles

Too much handling can make a pet reptile angry or aggressive. Smaller reptiles can also get injured if handled improperly. In some cases, it is best to coax a pet reptile into a plastic container inside its cage to pick it up. But there are times when owners will have to pick up their pet. Small lizards, such as geckos, should be held firmly, but lightly, in the palm of the hand. Many small lizards move very quickly, so a firm grip is important to prevent them from escaping. Never lift a pet reptile by its head or tail. That might injure or frighten it. Pet reptiles are likely to attack if frightened.

Small snakes, such as corn snakes, should be held on the neck directly behind the head, with the other hand supporting the middle of the snake's body. Tame snakes can be allowed to glide through the hands.

Big Reptiles

Large lizards, such as iguanas and monitors, can seriously hurt humans if provoked. Depending on the animal's size and nature, it may take more than one person to lift the lizard. The best way to lift a large lizard is to grip it firmly by the neck and use the other hand to support the animal's weight. Tuck the lizard's powerful tail under one arm to prevent it from lashing out. Human handlers should wear gloves because the lizard's skin is rough, and it might cut or scratch a person's skin.

It might also take more than one person to lift a large snake, such as a boa or python. One person should grasp the snake firmly by its neck, while another supports the snake's body. No matter how tame the snake, never drape it around someone's neck.

Some pythons can reach 30 feet (9 m) and weigh up to 300 pounds (136 kg).

Shedding skin is a slow process for a snake. It usually takes between one and two weeks from start to finish.

Shedding the Skin

All reptiles shed their skin as they grow. Snakes shed their skin in one piece, starting at the head and moving down the body. Lizards shed their skin in pieces. They remove bits of old skin by rubbing their body against a rough surface. Sometimes, they pull off their own skin and eat it! Even the hard-shelled turtles and tortoises shed their skin, but they do so very slowly.

Reptiles occasionally have a difficult time shedding their skin. This sometimes occurs if a reptile is ill. It is also common in new pet reptiles that have yet to feel comfortable in their new home. Placing a reptile in warm water helps soak the skin off. Gently rubbing a reptile with moist **sphagnum moss** can also help the shedding process. The moss softens the reptile's skin. Snakes often find it hard to shed the pieces of skin around their eyes. These pieces are called **spectacles**. They can be removed by gently dabbing around the snake's eyes with a piece of sticky tape. It is best to get an adult to do this so the animal does not get accidentally hurt.

Male or Female?

Finding out whether a pet reptile is male or female can be difficult. For many species, males and females look almost identical. For some lizards, however, it can be easy to tell them apart. Males often have colorful skin compared to the plain-colored skin of the females. Males may have a crest on their head or folds of skin called a **dewlap** hanging from their throat. These features attract females during the **breeding season**.

It is usually harder to tell male and female snakes apart. Generally, a male has a longer tail than the female. A male may also have a slight bulge where the tail joins the rest of the body. Additionally, the male may have two sets of **scales** on its tail instead of one. The only sure way of determining the sex of your pet is to have a reptile expert or a vet look at it.

A male iguana has a spiny crest and a beardlike dewlap.

A male giant tortoise follows a female during the breeding season in South Africa.

Ready to Mate

Only healthy reptiles can breed successfully. Sick reptiles will not usually reproduce. Reptile owners who want to breed their pets need to find out when and how often the animals can breed. Some species can breed every month, while others can only breed every few years. Extra care is often needed to ensure that the female reptile is ready to produce young. Some reptiles will need extra food to gain enough fat to breed. Others need to be given extra nutrients to ensure that their eggs and babies develop properly.

Mating Games

Many reptiles play games before they **mate**. These games are called **courtship**. Usually, the males compete for the females' attention. Some male lizards perform a courtship "dance" to impress the females. Other males change color or make the flaps of skin around their throat stand up. Still others fight for the right to mate. The winner mates with the female, and the loser slinks away. Snakes also fight for the right to mate. The male wins the contest by pinning down the other snake.

For some reptiles, mating lasts just a few minutes. For others, the process can take a few hours. During mating, male lizards often bite the female's neck, leaving small scars. When mating, a male and female snake move around together in the trees or on the ground.

A male adder lies on top of a female. In the wild, he finds her by scent.

A marginated tortoise hatches from its egg. This reptile is native to southern Europe.

Warming the Eggs

A few reptiles give birth to live young, but most lay eggs that hatch into new reptiles. In the wild, reptiles **incubate** their eggs by curling up around them or by burying them in the ground. Most pet reptiles do not incubate their eggs. Instead, the breeder removes the eggs and keeps them warm inside an incubator. The incubator is a special container that keeps the eggs at a constant temperature, usually 72 to 80°F (22 to 27°C). In some cases, it is best to leave the eggs in the reptile's enclosure. Gecko eggs are very sticky and should not be taken from their tank or cage. Instead, the eggs should be protected under a plastic container until they are ready to hatch.

Growing Up

Reptiles do not feed their babies milk like
mammals. However, some wild reptiles still
care for their young. The care of pet reptiles
usually falls to the human handler. Newly
hatched snakes do not need to feed until they
shed their skin for the first time. That may be
up to ten days after hatching. Some owners keep
very young reptiles in small plastic containers.
That makes it easier to feed them and keep an
eye on them. Young reptiles have different
nutritional needs from the adults. Often, young
pet reptiles need food supplements as well as
their normal food. Many young reptiles need
ultraviolet light to stay healthy, too.

This baby red-eared slider
might live to 40 years old.

Really big lizards are
best seen at a zoo or
a wildlife park.

Join the Club

Any new reptile owner should consider joining a reptile club. These organizations provide a lot of helpful information about reptile care. They are a good way to meet people who share an interest in looking after reptiles. People from reptile clubs usually meet once a month, and many clubs have a show, or expo, every year. Expos are a lot of fun. They are an ideal place to learn about reptiles. Reptile owners share advice, sell books and reptile food, and exhibit unusual reptiles that people would not usually see in pet stores.

Responsibilities

Owning a reptile—and making sure it does not escape—is a big responsibility. Responsible owners should spend time each day interacting with their pet. Owning or taking care of a pet reptile can be fun and very rewarding. Owners must be sure to have someone take care of their reptile whenever they go away.

Reptiles are some of the longest-lived animals. In 2006, a giant tortoise named Harriet died in an Australian zoo at about the age of 175 years! The life span of popular pet reptiles varies from five to ten years for chameleons and corn snakes to more than 30 or 40 years for pythons, turtles, and tortoises. Reptile owners need to be fully aware that their pet might live—and be a part of the family—for a very long time!

Words to Know

Abscesses	Pus-filled wounds.
Aquatic	Living in water.
Arboreal	Living in trees.
Bask	To sunbathe.
Breeding season	The time of the year when animals come together to mate.
Bungee cords	Elastic ropes that stretch to fasten or secure objects.
Captivity	When animals are kept by people rather than living in the wild.
Carnivores	Animals that eat mostly meat.
Courtship	When male and female animals try to impress each other before mating.
Dewlap	Folds of skin that hang from the throat of some male reptiles.
Diurnal	Active in the day.
Herbivores	Animals that eat only plants.
Hibernation	To spend winter in a deep sleeplike state.

Incubate	To keep eggs warm so they hatch into new animals.
Litter	Material used to line the bottom of a reptile's enclosure.
Mate	To come together to produce young.
Nocturnal	Active at night.
Omnivores	Animals that eat both plants and animals.
Parasites	Animals that live on or in other animals, feeding on their body tissues.
Predators	Animals that hunt other animals.
Scales	Thin, hard overlapping plates under a snake's skin that protect the snake.
Species	The scientific word for animals of the same kind that breed together.
Spectacles	Circular disks of skin around the eyes of a snake.
Sphagnum moss	A spongy plant, which can be used to help a pet reptile shed its skin.
Ultraviolet	A form of light that helps reptiles make essential nutrients. Ultraviolet light is given off by the Sun.

Find Out More

Books

Gaines, A. *Top 10 Reptiles and Amphibians for Kids*. Berkeley Heights, New Jersey: Enslow Publishers, Inc., 2008.

Gruber, B. *Reptile Style*. Pet's Point of View. Mankato, Minnesota: Compass Point Books, 2004.

Web sites

Jackson's Chameleons
www.nationalgeographic.com/coloringbook/chameleons.html
Print this picture and then color it in.

The Reptiles: Lizards
www.pbs.org/wnet/nature/reptiles/lizards_pets.html
Information about caring for pet lizards.

Index

52